I know I Can!
Bake a Cake

ANTHEA DAVIDSON-JARRETT
Illustrated by
Aldana Penayo
Published by EDUCATE THE GLOBE,
London, UK, 2022.

ISBN: 978-1-913804-00-8

Copyright © 2022 Educate The Globe Limited. All rights reserved. No part of this book is to be reprinted, copied or stored in retrieval systems of any type, except by written permission from the author. Part of this book may, however, be used only in reference to support related documents or subjects.

I know I can do it!

Please can I help?

I want to do it all by myself!

Please can I try?

Can you show me how?

I'm not too small,

I am ready right now!

It's my sister's birthday!

What cake shall we bake?

Daddy is a chef.

What is it he will make?

Cake with cream?

Cake with raisins?

Cake with chocolate?

Something amazing?

Big like a tree or

small like Kookie?

I don't know;

we shall see!

I am so excited!

The ingredients are here.

Wash our hands and

cover up our hair!

Put on our aprons -

get the bowls out!

Warm up the oven -

no time to stand about!

Nhalia doesn't eat eggs

so we will use flaxseeds.

To make the gooey gel

water's all we need!

Butter, flour and syrup;

mix them very well!

A pinch of vanilla essence!

Ooh! What a lovely smell.

Mix! Mix! Mix!

Until I start to scream!

"I'm tired! I'm tired!

Can we use the machine?"

It's stronger and faster!

It can hurt you so take care.

Daddy will help me

push the red button, there!

Round and round!

Mix the batter - so smooth.

Zoom! Zoom! Zoom!

Like when I run around my room!

Grease the baking tins.

Pour the batter in;...

check the oven's hot –

slide in the cake tin!

Watch the cake bake;

it keeps rising and rising!

Get the things ready

to make the icing!

Licking my fingers!

Pour the colouring in.

Stir! Stir! Stir!

Daddy watch what I'm doing!

The cake has finished baking;

oven gloves daddy wears.

The baking tin is very hot

so take time and take care!

Baking cakes

is so fun and it's so easy

like when I'm singing and counting:

1… 2… 3!

Or when I sing and say

my ABCs.

Now I know I can do it

for anybody!

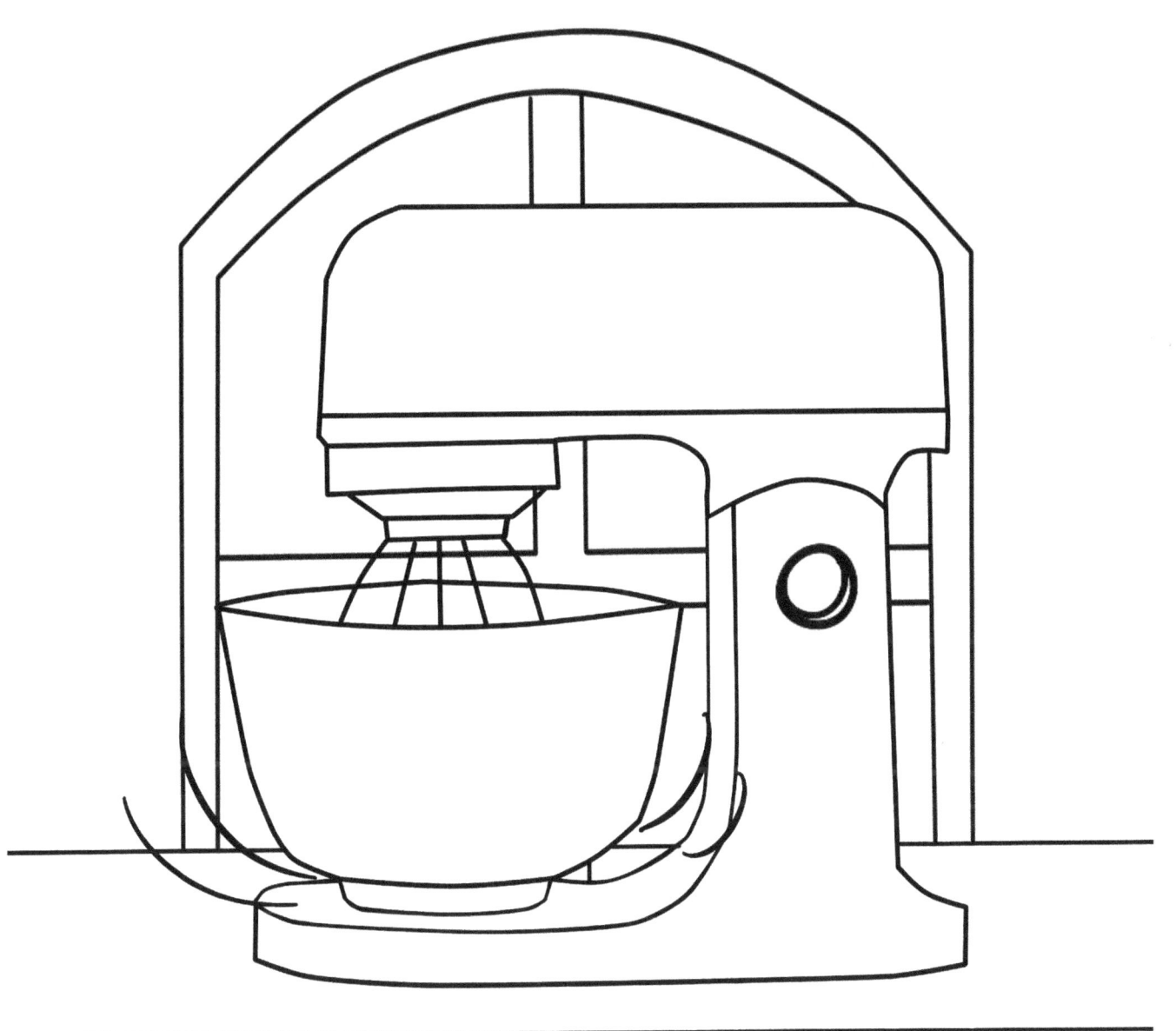

www.ingramcontent.com/pod-product-compliance
Lightning Source LLC
Chambersburg PA
CBHW041244240426
43670CB00027B/2989